Italy Travel Guide

51 Amazing Things to Do in Italy

51 Amazing Things

Copyright © 2017 by 51 Amazing things

All rights reserved.

Publisher's Disclaimer

This book is for informational purposes only.

Printed in the U.S.A

Contents

An Introduction On Traveling To Italy	5
Chapter 1 – Rome	7
#1 Visit The Colosseum	8
#2 Attend Mass At The Pantheon	10
#3 Throw A Coin Into The Trevi Fountain	11
#4 See Where Rome Was Formed At Palatine Hill	12
#5 Explore The Old Roman Forum	14
#6 Be Like A Local At Trastevere	14
#7 Shop Sunday Mornings At The Porta Portese	15
#8 Walk Along The Appian Way	17
#9 Visit The Market At The Campo De' Fiori	18
#10 Listen For The Cannon At Gianicolo Hill	19
#11 Travel To The Top Of The Altare Della Patria	20
Chapter 2 – Milan	22
#12 Honor The Past At The Piazza Del Duomo	22
#13 Find Fashions At The Galleria Vittorio Emanuele Ii	23

#14 See The Last Supper At The Santa Maria Delle Grazie — 25

#15 See Opera At La Scala — 27

#16 Learn About Da Vinci At The Museo Mazionale Scienza E Tecnologia — 28

#17 See The Action At The Borsa Italiana — 29

Chapter 3 – Florence — 31

#18 Enjoy A Free Hour At The Loggia Del Lanzi — 31

#19 Admire Michelangelo's David At The Galleria Dell'accademia — 32

#20 Be Inspired At The Boboli Gardens — 34

#21 Learn About Art At The Uffizi Gallery — 35

#22 Look Up The Roof Of The Florence Cathedral — 37

Brunelleschi's Cathedral

Chapter 4 – Vatican City — 39

#23 Make A Pilgrimage St. Peter's Basilica — 40

#24 Look Up To The Ceiling Of The Sistine Chapel — 42

#25 Visit The Raphael Rooms At The Palace Of The Vatican — 44

#26 Learn About Ancient Italy At The Etruscan Museum — 45

#27 Review The Books At The Vatican Library — 47

#28 Review The Gallery Of Maps At The Belvedere Courtyard — 47

Chapter 5 – Turin — 49

#29 See The Shroud Of Turin At The Cathedral Of Saint John The Baptist — 49

#30 Enjoy The Show At The National Museum Of Cinema — 51

#31 Explore The History Of Automobiles At The Museo Dell'automobile Di Torino — 52

#32 Explore Ancient Egypt At The Museo Egizio — 54

Chapter 6 – Venice — 56

#33 Enjoy A Ride Under The Rialto Bridge At The Grand Canal — 56

#34 Walk Along The Bridge Of Sighs — 58

#35 Enter Doge's Palace On The Waterfront — 59

#36 Explore A Napoleonic Site In The Academy Gallery — 60

#37 Visit The Markets At St. Mark's Square — 61

#38 Watch A Show At The Teatro La Fenice — 63

Chapter 7 – Naples — 65

#39 Explore The Past At The Naples National Archeological Museum — 65

#40 Go Shopping At Christmas Alley — 66

#41 Shop At The Via Caracciolo E Lungomare Promenade — 68

#42 See The Veiled Christ At The Sanservo Chapel Museum — 69

Chapter 8 – Verona 71

#43 Experience Shakespeare's Inspiration At The Casa Di Giulietta 71

#44 Get To The Top Of The Torre Dei Lamberti 73

#45 See Opera At The Arena Di Verona 74

Chapter 9 – Other Places Around Italy 76

#46 Enjoy The Wines Of Piedmont 76

#47 Visit The Island Of Sicily 78

#48 See Where Napoleon Lived On Elba 79

#49 Watch Your Step At The Leaning Tower Of Pisa 80

#50 Climb Up One Of The Mountains At The Pennine Alps 82

#51 See The Active Volcano On Stromboli 83

Bonus - #52 Enjoy The Nightlife Of Capri 84

Bonus - #53 Ski At One Of The Northern Resorts 85

Bonus -#54 Relax At The Waters Around Lake Garda 87

Bonus - #55 See The Ruins Of Pompeii 89

Conclusion 91

An Introduction on Traveling to Italy

Italy is a fascinating country in the world which deserves to be explored. The country is home to centuries of culture and history. From the beautiful architectural wonders of Italy to its many public spaces and museums, the country is distinct. Of course, there are plenty of great foods for people to enjoy and some unique shopping spots too.

This guide is all about looking at some of the appealing things you will find while in Italy. There are dozens of great activities worth partaking in while you are in Italy.

Check out the many great cities around Italy plus some of the beautiful countryside spots. The coastal and mountain regions are worth looking into.

Look at the strong religious influences that the country is famous for. Many of these influences come from the Catholic Church. Considering that Italy is where Vatican City is located, it is no surprise that much of the country is heavily based off of religious values.

From the performing arts to modern history, many places bring out the best of Italy. There are also some places so iconic and prominent that no trip to the country would ever be complete without going to those spots.

The points you will read about here include many things relating to what makes Italy one of the most dynamic countries in the world. There are so many activities to find around Italy that it might be tough for you to complete them all. This guide is simply designed to give you ideas of what you could experience and enjoy while you are traveling around this vast and grand country.

Chapter 1 – Rome

Rome is one of the most historic cities in the world. The city has its roots in 753 BC according to the famed legend of Romulus and Remus. The twin brothers formed the city after building a significant army. Romulus named the city after himself and determined the location not long after Remus was killed.

Over the years Rome developed into a massive city with its empire that spread along Europe, the Middle East and Northern Africa in the second century AD. Today the Roman Empire may be a thing of the past, but the rich history and culture of the city persist to this day.

It is no secret that there are many things worth doing while in Rome. It is a city you will never forget.

#1 Visit the Colosseum

People often reference the Colosseum as the most iconic place in all of Rome. The striking and distinct look of the Colosseum retains many of the features that were introduced thousands of years ago. The engineering features of the Colosseum make it a highly influential space that people continue to study and review to this day.

Built around 70 AD, the Colosseum is an oval amphitheater made with sand and concrete. It was a prominent venue that hosted gladiatorial contests, animal hunting events, and even public executions. The floor even has a wide opening for flooding so the Colosseum could host demonstration sea battles.

Much of the Colosseum is in ruins as some parts were reused for other construction projects around Rome. Today the main body of the

Colosseum persists and even has numerous tunnels and other intricate features laid out all over the place. Walk through this stunning wonder of the modern world and see the intricate design of the venue.

Go to the floor and see the detailed layout that was used for securing weapons, gladiators, animals and much more. The flooring setup is called the hypogeum and features tunnels that lead to the main competition surface. The layout is a true marvel featuring a carefully planned organization that includes enough rooms for all the people who would have competed.

Travel along the individual concourses where spectators would have walked along to get to their seats. Look at the arches around the outside and see how they are nearly identical to each other.

The Colosseum is one of the best-preserved ruins in all of Rome. It is a worthwhile site that is truly memorable.

#2 Attend Mass at the Pantheon

The Pantheon is a church noted for its large columns. Built in the early second century AD, the Pantheon is a circular building which features Corinthian columns around its front entrance. Much of the building has been perfectly preserved.

The concrete dome features multiple indentations around its body. A circular hole in the middle of the dome allows light to shine through. This is the largest concrete dome in the world that does not require any support features.

Several marble interior accents highlight the Pantheon. From the detailed multi-colored floors to the strong columns, the marble accents inside the building are designed with strong bodies.

See the tombs where many key figures in the nation's history are buried. The nineteenth century kings Vittorio Emanuele II and Umberto I are both buried at the Pantheon as well as Queen Margherita.

Catholic masses are held at the Pantheon on Sundays and major holy days. The masses operate on classic Vatican standards. The Latin language is utilized along with traditional incantations. These are clearly different from what you might have seen in a more traditional modern mass, but this brings about a great look into the history of the faith.

#3 Throw a Coin Into the Trevi Fountain

Rome has its share of fountains, but none are quite as famous as the Trevi Fountain. The eighteenth century stone fountain is a massive Baroque work of art.

Oceanus, the Roman god of water, is the central figure in the statue. See as he looks towards onward as numerous waterfalls move out from the middle. The central waterfall is the largest of them all.

The papal coat of arms can be found at the top end of the fountain. A few bas reliefs around the body show how the aqueducts of Rome were formed.

The fountain features prominently in many films and was even highlighted on a postage stamp issued by the Italian government. The tall body of the fountain makes for a more visibly intriguing surface.

It is widely believed that anyone who tosses a coin into the fountain will return to Rome one day. You must throw your coin in with your right hand over your left shoulder as this is a tradition. Coins are regularly gathered by city officials to provide food to the city's neediest residents.

#4 See Where Rome Was Formed at Palatine Hill

Not all historical parts of Rome are preserved like the Colosseum or Pantheon. The city does respect its extensive history and has kept a few wide open spots fully protected. These include regions where many important buildings and sites critical to the foundation and development of the city were located.

See the original center of Rome as you travel to Palatine Hill. The region is situated on the eastern end of the Tiber and is just west of the Colosseum.

Much of Rome's early history traces back to Palatine Hill. See where emperor Augustus lived as the frescoes of his home add a beautiful look to the region. Notice the retaining walls around the region that protected the area.

The footprints from many older buildings are around the walkways of Palatine Hill. Remains of the Temples of Cybele and Apollo Palatinus still stand today.

The Arch of Septimus Severus welcomes people into the region. The Temple of Saturn still has many of its tall columns standing to this day. The temple dates back to around the fourth century AD. The eight existing columns support a large base with an inscription at the top. It was used as a place to honor the god Saturn.

#5 Explore the Old Roman Forum

The Roman Forum is a large plaza that features the ruins of many old buildings from the city's early days. Located not too far from Palatine, the Roman Forum is an area where trials and speeches were held in the city's earliest days.

Much of the forum features ruins from the old buildings that housed important governmental activities. Look for the Temples of Concord, Vesta, and Caesar. Some of the altars surrounding these temples are still standing.

Although many of the buildings have since deteriorated, the foundations and footprints of many of these spots are still standing. Notice when looking around the forum that the buildings are made of marble and stone materials that had become weathered but still retain the colors and tones they held when their buildings first existed.

#6 Be Like a Local at Trastevere

There are many neighborhoods around Rome, but none are quite as distinct as Trastevere. The region is right on the western end of the Tiber and is home to many prominent dining spaces. The promenade along the river provides guests with some of the best views of the city.

The region features some of the most appealing Italian restaurants around. These places focus on authentic recipes and ingredients. The foods are particularly cheaper than what people might find in other regions. Visitors have particularly heralded how the region is not too crowded and offers a more natural look at what Rome is all about.

The Piazza Santa Maria is one prominent place in Trastevere that doubles as an important meeting space for people in the region. The church features a series of gilded windows and some of the most elaborate mosaic art pieces in Rome.

The region is peaceful and relaxing. The quaint appeal of Trastevere makes it a must-see place to visit in Rome.

#7 Shop Sunday Mornings At the Porta Portese

The art of the flea market is on full display at the Porta Portese in Rome. Take home a highly unique souvenir at this market. However, the shopping space is not too accessible as the hours of operation are extremely limited. Such standards are in place to create a more controlled environment where only the best artisans and retailers can have their own stations at the Porta Portese.

Porta Portese is a market that is open every Sunday morning. The community setting focuses on local products with a tight-knit environment all the way through. The standards for being included in the market are high.

Art pieces are available for sale including both reprints of classic works and more distinct modern pieces. Clothing products from many local fabrics experts and fashion houses are available too. Most of the clothes for sale are new although there are a few places that sell used options too. But those clothes are made with high standards in mind.

Books and antiques are also available. Some of the antiques include lookalikes that are designed to have gem or crystal-like qualities.

#8 Walk Along the Appian Way

Take a bit of time walking along the Appian Way while in Rome. The road is close to forty miles in length although most parts of the road have been fully restored and are open for walking.

The Appian Way links Rome to Brindisi. The road is where military forces would move between cities.

Some parts of the Appian Way feature the same stones and mortar that were applied around 300 BC. A few spaces have worn out as the cement materials have broken down.

Travel along the road to see many spaces where important moments in Rome's history took place. See the wide paths were military marches were regularly held. Look for a few of the fields were Spartacus and many of his followers were executed at in 71 BC.

#9 *Visit the Market at the Campo de' Fiori*

Campo de' Fiori is a public square which features social and commercial activities. This place in Rome has held importance for the city since at least the fourteenth century. The region continues to be a popular space for markets. Visit the daily market and see what foods are available.

Local produce products, wines, arts, and clothing are available for sale through various vendors at the Campo de' Fiori. Find some of the authentic olive oils and balsamic vinegar produced locally as well as freshly baked bread that goes well with these oils.

Observe the statue of Giordano Bruno at the square. The famed philosopher was burned at the square in 1600 and has long since been heralded as a person who promoted the freedom of thought around Italy.

The market is open during the daytime hours, but it is best to come out here during the earliest parts of the day. The market is not likely to be crowded during the early morning hours. The region is a popular place that highlights a number of intriguing features.

#10 Listen For the Cannon at Gianicolo Hill

For the best views of Rome, go west of the river to Gianicolo Hill. See the Vatican and Trastevere regions of the city from high atop the hill. The viewpoint from the region is very clear as you will notice everything the city has to offer. Views of the Tiber are particularly noticeable as you see how the river curves its way and divides the city up.

Learn about the reunification of Italy in the nineteenth century at Gianicolo Hill. Numerous busts and statues of people who were critical to bringing Italy back together after centuries of political strife are featured around the region. The most prominent of these is the statue of Giuseppe Garibaldi on horseback. The famed general was beloved and essential for his support over the reunification of the land.

Come out to Gianicolo at noon to hear the cannon on site fire. The shot of the cannon at noon is held as a tribute to the unity of Italy and the power of the country. This tradition has been ongoing since the mid-nineteenth century and is the only time when the peaceful and tranquil scenes of Gianicolo Hill break.

#11 *Travel to the Top of the Altare Della Patria*

The Altare Della Patria, or Altar of the Fatherland, is a monument dedicated to the first kind of a fully unified Italy, Victor Emmanuel. Built around the turn of the twentieth century over the course of nearly forty years, the top area features an observation deck. Look from more than 200 feet above ground at the vast cityscape of Rome.

Observe the immense amount of detail surrounding the altar. See the large statues of warriors and horses on the top while many columns adorn the middle part of the altar. The building's rectangular design prompts many to refer to it as the "wedding cake building."

See the Italian unification museum at the base. Learn about how Rome became the capital of Italy in 1871 and how many political and social movements developed to get the many states of the Italian peninsula back together.

Honor Rome's military past at the Tomb of the Unknown Soldier. Situated at the base of the altar, the tomb is surrounded by a massive statue of the goddess Roma. The remains of an unknown Italian soldier from World War I are protected by guards twenty-four hours a day.

Chapter 2 – Milan

Situated in the northern end of Italy in the Lombardy region, the city of Milan is truly dynamic. The city was critical to the reunification of Italy as people in Milan rebelled against Austrian rule in 1848.

Milan continues to grow as a thriving economic hub. It is also one of the most important cities in the fashion world. The city is home to a few museums that promote many of the most important figures in the art and science world. Look at what Milan has to offer as you explore the region.

#12 Honor the Past at the Piazza del Duomo

See the incredible architecture of the Piazza del Duomo while in Milan. The plaza has numerous developments dating back to the fourteenth century.

The Milan Cathedral is the main highlight of the plaza. The Gothic cathedral features an immense amount of detail. The main spires are around 350 feet in height and feature brick and Candoglia marble materials. The building is so detailed that the construction process for the cathedral went from 1386 all the way to 1965.

Visit the statue of Saint Bartholomew inside the cathedral. See the many sarcophagi where some of Italy's former archbishops are buried in. Look for the 225-rank pipe organ that operates as the largest in the country.

Look for the Royal Palace of Milan, a former government seat and walk along its neoclassical staircase. Visit the museum highlighting artifacts from the Napoleonic era and the Restoration period.

#13 Find Fashions At the Galleria Vittorio Emanuele II
Milan is home to many fashion houses that produce the finest and most influential clothing

products in today's industry. The Galleria Vittorio Emanuele II shopping mall brings many of them together as they sell their finest wares.

The Galleria opened in 1877 and is one of the oldest shopping malls in the world. The building's spacious design is influential as various modern malls have been designed with more walking room just like what the Galleria has.

Look up to see the massive glass and iron roof. The arched design of the roof allows natural light to come in while lanterns provide illumination at night.

Shop for fashions from many of the world's top labels at the Galleria. Various Italian fashion houses sell their wares directly to the people here. A few international names from around Europe and North America also have stores where they also sell high-end fashions.

The fashions for sale include options for men and women alike. From the hottest shoes to the finest dresses, many contemporary products are available. Do be prepared to spend a large amount of money on fashions here though. The high-end nature of the products for sale makes it hard for people to enjoy good things.

Still, the shops are all available for the public to view. Check out the beautiful fashions to see what trends have come about in the industry.

Review the rooms and features of the Town House Galleria hotel inside the Galleria. It is the only hotel in the world with a certified 7-star rating. Many of the suites around the hotel overlook the shopping area.

#14 See the Last Supper at the Santa Maria Delle Grazie

Various buildings around Milan house some of the most important art pieces that have ever been made. These include spots that feature artwork from many centuries ago. One of the places to look for is an old church that houses an iconic work.

The Santa Maria Delle Grazie, or Holy Mary of Grace, church is a Gothic building from the fifteenth century. The beautiful nave features several floral artistic accents. Much of the building features walls that were rebuilt following an aerial bombing in 1943.

But the most noteworthy feature of this Milan church comes from how it is home to the Last

Supper, the famed mural painted by Leonardo da Vinci.

Located inside the rectory, the iconic 1494 painting depicts the Last Supper of Jesus as depicted in the Gospel of John. The painting went through a massive restoration process during the late twentieth century.

Look around the rectory and see how the famed mural fits in with the rest of the room. Notice the intricate detail that da Vinci put into his work. Identify the various references to the number three scattered around the work. That number is representative of the Holy Trinity, one of the most important concepts of the Christian faith.

Much of the original painting is hard to identify though. The restoration process was especially extreme due to how the painting had worn out over the centuries. Even with this, an immense amount of work was put into ensuring that the painting would survive and continue to impress people to this day.

Make sure you get your ticket to see the Last Supper early. People who visit the house are limited to spending only 15 minutes with the picture. The time limit is regulated quite well, what with the demand to see this being so high.

#15 *See Opera at La Scala*

Enjoy the fine arts while in Milan. Operatic performances are essential as they reflect Italian culture. La Scala is one place that you can see shows at.

La Scala is an opera house which hosts numerous operatic performances. Both Italian and international performers alike come to La Scala to perform regularly. The theater has a full schedule throughout the entire year.

Built in 1778, La Scala is an outstanding venue for opera. The interior includes several tiers of seating space while an elaborate chandelier provides light from the center of the ceiling.

Many new opera productions take place at La Scala every year although performances of classic shows can be found as well. Tickets can be relatively hard to come by although the venue is available for tours during the daytime.

The opera events especially highlight the history of the art form. La Scala focuses on both traditional and modern opera productions. You will be impressed at how well the people at La Scala can perform various operatic productions.

#16 Learn About da Vinci at the Museo Mazionale Scienza e Tecnologia

Milan is home to a museum dedicated to Leonardo da Vinci. The Museo Mazionale Scienza e Tecnologia is situated inside an old monastery building.

Various exhibits include devices and machines that were designed and devised by da Vinci. Modern machines that are directly influenced by his work are on display in the museum.

Individual sections of the museum are about musical instruments, transportation devices, raw materials, and astronomy. Many of the innovations da Vinci developed in his lifetime are highlighted in these sections. A lute maker's workshop from around the seventeenth century is also in the museum. The full recreation of this space is designed with an entertaining look.

The museum illustrates the importance of da Vinci's work and highlights how well technology has evolved over the years. The features of the museum make it one of the more distinct places to visit while in the city.

#17 See the Action at the Borsa Italiana

Milan is an important business and economic center in Italy. The Borsa Italiana is a part of the city that highlights how valuable Milan truly is.

Watch as people head to the Borsa Italiana on weekdays to trade stocks and share financial data. See how the technology works around the stock exchange to see how trades are processed. The intricate and busy nature of the stock exchange makes it one of the more intriguing sites to look for while in Milan.

The stocks traded at the Borsa Italiana include ones offered by various companies from all around the country in many industries. Support for international trades is offered as well. Check out the beautiful columns on the front façade of the main building as well. The property that the exchange is based out of has been in operation since the early nineteenth century.

Regular trading activities are held on weekdays. Visit the Borsa Italiana to learn more about what goes on at such an intriguing place as this.

Chapter 3 – Florence

Florence is a famous city in the Tuscany region of Italy. The city was a key part of the Renaissance as Italy grew into a more powerful and influential country. It is especially vital for its artistic influence as the country's most important Renaissance painters often produced their works here.

Florence is especially prominent as a city that offers numerous art-related attractions. The museums around the city highlight some of the most important paintings ever produced.

#18 Enjoy a Free Hour at the Loggia del Lanzi

One of the greatest issues people have about visiting Italy is that every attraction costs money to get into. This is not the case with the Loggia del Lanzi.

The Loggia del Lanzi is an open-air museum space that is free to the public. Spend about an hour around this museum built in the fourteenth century and see many iconic sculptures on display. The famed Giambologna work, the Rape of the Sabines, is the highlight of the museum.

Look for the four trefoils carved by Agnolo Gaddi near the arches of the space. Each of these trefoils represents one of the four cardinal virtues. The virtues of Fortitude, Temperance, Justice, and Prudence, are all on display. Each has its own pose and symbolic features.

Head to the nearby Fountain of Neptune and enjoy a drink from one of the local cafes nearby. The fountain is right alongside the Loggia del Lanzi. Get there early as the area tends to get rather busy in the middle of the day.

#19 Admire Michelangelo's David at the Galleria dell'Accademia

Michelangelo's iconic early-sixteenth century statue David remains of the most important statues in world history. The statue shows the Biblical figure around the time when he decided to face off against Goliath. The statue has been analyzed for centuries in terms of the proportions of David's body and what they mean. From David's eyes looking towards Rome to the large head and hands and even down to the small genitals, many features of the statue deserve to be analyzed for meaning.

Observe David for yourself at the Galleria dell'Accademia as you are in Florence. See the intense detail that Michelangelo puts into David's muscles and tissues. Learn about how the statue was seen as a symbol of resistance against the values of the Medici family.

Look at how the powerful marble surface of the statue stands out from everything else in the room. The strong appearance has survived for centuries even as it has been moved from one place to the next and was even attacked at one point in the late twentieth century.

Tickets are available for the museum although you would have to schedule a specific time of day for when you can see David. Check out the other works around the museum while waiting for your time to see the statue. See the Florentine Gothic paintings that line up around the body of the museum. It is true that none of the features around the museum are quite as iconic or noteworthy as David but the place itself still deserves to be noticed for its intriguing features.

#20 Be Inspired At the Boboli Gardens

Take in a bit of time away from the busy sounds and sights of Florence and relax at the Boboli Gardens. The garden space was first laid out in the sixteenth century. The gardens feature many landmark accents that were commonly found in Italian gardens at the time including added stone accents, small temple spaces, and various statues all around.

Visit the Isolotto fountain around the southwestern end of the gardens. This large fountain blends in perfectly with the surrounding landscape.

Look for the many sculptures scattered around the gardens. Giambologna's Bathing Venus is one such sculpture to see. Notice how Venus appears to be caressing herself in acknowledgment of her natural beauty.

The Boboli Gardens are carefully landscaped and cared for throughout the year. You will notice this through the clean archways and perfect shapes of the many shrubs all around the gardens.

As you walk along, head to the northern end for a perfect view of Florence. See how the Arno divides the two halves of the city from your vantage point.

#21 Learn About Art at the Uffizi Gallery

See the original works of various iconic Italian artists at the Uffizi Gallery. Many of the works come from the house of Medici, a former ruling family that collected art. The Medicis were prominent patrons who supported many artistic efforts for generations and collected art pieces to preserve them. Much of what the family held is on display for today's audiences to see.

Walk around the elaborate interior of the museum and see the art pieces from Italian Renaissance artists. See various classic works like da Vinci's Annunciation, Botticelli's Birth of Venus and Rembrandt's Self-Portrait. Additional paintings and sculptures from Giotto, Duccio, Titian, Raphael, and Caravaggio are also on display.

Enjoy the beauty of the outdoor courtyard located between the two main wings of the museum. The meeting space has a view of the Arno River.

It is best for you to get tickets to visit the museum online and to schedule a time to visit. The museum is very popular, but there are limits as to how many people can get into it at a given time.

#22 Look Up the Roof of the Florence Cathedral

When the Florence Cathedral was built in the early fourteenth century, it was built to show how important the city had become. It was to be larger than the building which came before it.

Today the Florence Cathedral continues to dominate the Florence skyline. At around 370 feet in height, the building is distinguished by its large dome. The red tiles along the outside of the dome add to the distinct look of the building.

The dome is important to the development of Italian architecture as it does away with the Gothic buttresses many other properties used. A singular concrete shell was used to create a sturdy body. The design continues to persist to this day even though the precise formula for the concrete material has been lost. The inside part of the roof includes a series of murals featuring many figures inspired by the Bible.

Look at the bronze doors at the front part of the cathedral. These are embellished with scenes of the Madonna. The designs include this figure and her child and take a heavy amount of inspiration from the work of Raphael.

The Florence Cathedral is not necessarily as famous as the Sistine Chapel, another point to read about in this guide. But it still features a distinct series of great points that make it an important place to visit.

Chapter 4 – Vatican City

Vatican City is technically its own country when all is considered. It is a city-state right in the middle of Rome. At about 109 acres in size, it is a distinct place. But it is also one of the most important places in the world when its value is put into play.

Vatican City is the home of the Roman Catholic Church. This is where the Pope resides. It is also home to many intriguing sights that deserve to be explored.

Make some time in Vatican City while you are in Rome. Head past the walls that surround Vatican City and see everything the area has to offer. The city is truly one of a kind as it illustrates the importance of the Catholic faith to millions around the world to this day.

#23 Make a Pilgrimage St. Peter's Basilica

St. Peter's Basilica is a critical pilgrimage site for those of the Catholic faith. This massive church is believed to be where Saint Peter is buried. Peter was one of Jesus' apostles and served as the first Pope from 30 to 67 AD. He served as the Pope longer than any other person in history.

The basilica marks an important moment in Vatican history. The construction of this building in the sixteenth century was funded through the sale of indulgences. This led to Martin Luther starting the Protestant Reformation.

Enter the basilica and see the massive interior. The nave is nearly 700 feet long and 500 feet wide. Around 60,000 people can fit inside.

See the dome designed by Michelangelo. Head up the stairs to the roof to get a closer view of the dome before you head outdoors for a beautiful look at the public square situated outside the building. See the Pieta sculpture by Michelangelo inside the building.

Get your tickets early to visit the papal tombs in the bottom part of the basilica. The tomb of Saint Peter is inside the burial area. Many other Popes are buried here with numerous statues accompanying their final resting sites. Be sure you reserve tickets soon as there are extreme limits over how many people can visit the tombs. About 250 people can visit them on a typical day. This is out of respect for the burial sites.

There are times when the Pope will directly address the crowd. These include important times on the Catholic calendar. It would be difficult to actually get into the basilica itself. Therefore, the Pope will contact the crowd direct from a much larger position that overlooks the massive courtyard outside the basilica. This is also where the new Pope is introduced when the conclave has determined who that Pope will be.

Seek out a good position in the courtyard during such special times. The Pope's words are followed by many, so it is no surprise that people from all corners of the world will come out to this place to hear him speak.

#24 Look Up to the Ceiling of the Sistine Chapel

The Sistine Chapel is a large hall built in the late fifteenth century. The building is the domestic chapel for the Pope. It is also where the conclave that elects a new Pope is held in following the death of the prior one.

The chapel is a place where many masses are still held, but the most noteworthy feature of the chapel is its intricate ceiling. There are numerous paintings from Botticelli, Perugino, and Ghirlandaio around the ceiling.

But the most important part of the ceiling comes from the many scenes of the Bible that were painted by Michelangelo. The Renaissance master painted several scenes on the ceiling including many from the Book of Genesis. These were all painted by Michelangelo from 1508 to 1512.

The nine scenes from the Book of Genesis portrayed including his iconic scenes of the creation of Adam and Eve and their eventual banishment from Eden. The creation of the universe and God's creation of the sun and planets plus the division of light from darkness are also featured. The three stories of Noah round out the main panels.

Look at the twelve prophetic features included in the ceiling. See Jonah right above the altar.

Go outside and look for the chimney at the top part of the chapel. This is important when the conclave meets as it is used to signal how the conclave operates. When black smoke comes out, it means the conclave has not chosen a new Pope just yet. When white smoke appears, the conclave has found a Pope and that person will be introduced outside the basilica very soon.

Some masses are held at the Sistine Chapel, but the building itself is often open to the public during much of the day. Come inside and take a look but try to get a view of the ceiling from as many angles as possible. The intense detail around the entire chapel makes for a nice look all around.

#25 Visit the Raphael Rooms At the Palace of the Vatican

The Palace of the Vatican is an important building in the city. This is where the Pope lives. The Papal Apartments, Vatican Museums, and Vatican Library are all included here. The building itself includes many attractive places worth visiting, but the most beautiful spaces to see are the Raphael Rooms.

The Raphael Rooms are four individual rooms open to the public outside the Papal Apartments. These four rooms include frescoes painted by Raphael plus many of his associates.

The four rooms include several important scenes of history. The Room of Constantine shows images of Constantine the Roman Emperor and how the Christian faith won over paganism. Other rooms depict the lives of many popes who served in the past.

Notice the intense detail in each of these Renaissance paintings. See how the individual art pieces display important scenes of history that were vital to the development of the faith.

#26 Learn About Ancient Italy At the Etruscan Museum

The Etruscan civilization was a wealthy part of Italy which began around 768 BC and moved along until the fourth century BC when it was assimilated into the Roman Republic. It is one of the more intriguing civilizations in recorded history. The group had its own currency and language and was heavily influenced by Greek and Celtic cultures.

Not much is fully known about the Etruscans. But what is known is on display at the Etruscan Museum in Vatican City. The museum was formed in the late nineteenth century to analyze the history of early Italy.

See some of the many intriguing artifacts from the Etruscan civilization in the eighteen rooms around the museum. Look for old Etruscan graves and other items that have been excavated including pieces of art. The discoveries give the viewer an idea of what Etruscans thought the afterlife was like.

View the Sarcophagus of the Spouses, a terracotta sarcophagus produced in the sixth century BC. This life-sized art piece features a man and woman reclining together at a banquet in the afterlife. The work is an appealing look into the history of the Etruscan people as it shows that women were respected a little more than they were in other cultures at the time. Note how the two people appear to have positive looks on their face, a symbol of how death was not something for Etruscans to mourn but rather to celebrate.

Look at the other art pieces from the time on display. The Centaur of Vulci is one iconic piece that is distinct for displaying a proper anatomical look at one of the more familiar creatures of Greek mythology, another clue at how Greek culture was vital to the development of Etruscan society.

#27 Review the Books At the Vatican Library

See the many important books on display at the Vatican Library. It has a massive hall featuring at least 80,000 manuscripts and 25,000 hand-written books dating back as far as 1450, the year the library was founded. Thousands of other documents from before then are also on display although it is not fully clear as to what the final number is, what with there being so many.

See many of the important books on display including old Gospels and Biblical codices. Many pages from these works are on display.

Do not expect to check out any books or even to review individual ones though. The books at the Vatican Library are regularly analyzed and studied by historians and scholars. They review these works to get an idea of how society and culture have evolved over the years. The work that scholars put in at the library is important to understanding the evolution of society at the time.

#28 Review the Gallery of Maps at the Belvedere Courtyard

The Belvedere Courtyard is an attractive space in the Vatican that connects the main palace with much of the common area. One of the most distinct features you will see while in the courtyard is the Gallery of Maps. It is the world's largest pictorial map display.

The Gallery of Maps was produced in the late sixteenth century through the support of Pope Gregory XIII. Walk through the gallery to see many topographic maps of Italy. The maps have been painted on the walls by Ignazio Danti, a famed Italian astronomer.

See the 40 individual panels of the gallery measuring at around 400 feet in length. Notice the incredible accuracy that Danti put into each of his panels. It is estimated that about 80 percent of the maps are accurate.

The panels are divided up by the Apennines. Look for the individual cities of Italy as they were depicted at the time and see how detailed the mountain ranges and bodies of water around the country are listed. The maps are detailed and influential to understanding cartography.

Chapter 5 – Turin

Northwestern Italy is home to Turin, one of the most dynamic cities in the country. Visit the city to experience history come to life.

Turin is famous for being the first capital of a fully unified Italy. It was named the capital in 1861.

The city is popular for being a vital cultural center of Italy. It is home to many quality restaurants and chocolatiers. It is also where much of Italy's film industry developed in the early part of the twentieth century. Turin is also a prominent sporting center of Italy that hosted the 2006 Winter Olympics.

Many tourists often overlook the city, but it is an essential place to visit in the city. Take a look at many of the features around the city and see what makes it an essential stop on any tour of Italy.

#29 See the Shroud of Turin at the Cathedral of Saint John the Baptist

The Shroud of Turin is one of the most important artifacts in the Catholic faith. This linen cloth features the image of a man who many believe is Jesus of Nazareth. It is also believed to be the shroud that Jesus was buried in following his death. Although the Catholic Church has neither denounced nor endorsed the cloth, followers of the church continue to hold the shroud in extremely high regard.

There has been a great debate over the years as to whether this is what was used in the burial of Jesus. Radiocarbon dating suggests that the shroud dates back to the Middle Ages. Meanwhile, several physical features of the shroud suggest that it could have dated back to Jesus' death, what with the cloth featuring markings of punctures around the scalp, one wrist having been pierced and blood having streamed down areas that Jesus' arms would have handled it.

One point is for certain though – the Shroud of Turin is widely respected as a key connection between the history of the Bible and the present. While in Turin, travel to the Cathedral of Saint John the Baptist to see this intriguing cloth.

Look at the immense detail of this nearly 15-foot-long linen. See the blood marks and other features around its body. Spot how travertine limestone surfaces had stuck around the cloth; this surface is identical to what was found in the area that Jesus is believed to have been buried at.

Do check with the cathedral to see if the shroud is on display before you attend. The shroud is regularly placed on display for the public to see although sometimes it is taken back into a private area for further analysis. Considering the strong mystery and intrigue surrounding the shroud, there is always the chance that it might not be on display at a given time.

#30 *Enjoy the Show at the National Museum of Cinema*

Learn about the development of cinema at the National Museum of Cinema in Turin. The museum is right inside the Mole Antonelliana building and features an extensive array of artifacts from the history of film.

See individual wings that highlight the processes that go into making films. Learn about individual film genres and how they have developed over the years.

The museum does have many highlights relating to Italian cinema, but films from all corners of the world are represented here.

See some of the old film posters, film stocks and other portraits of actors and movie crews. Look at some of the old shoes and other fashions once owned by Marilyn Monroe. Observe a typewriter that Woody Allen used to write many of his iconic films. See the bright red scarf once owned by Federico Fellini. Review the detailed design model for one of the dinosaurs featured in Jurassic Park.

Individual items used in many famous films are on display. Various masks used in the Star Wars and Planet of the Apes film series are visible. See the original printed screenplay to the Godfather and Boris Karloff's mask bust for his work on Frankenstein.

#31 Explore the History of Automobiles at the Museo dell'Automobile di Torino

Turin is famous for being the capital of the Italian auto industry. Fiat, Alfa Romeo, and Lancia are all based out of Turin. Those companies and many others are proudly represented at the Museo dell'Automobile di Torino.

Visit the museum and see many iconic vehicles on display. Hundreds of cars are featured at the museum including not only Italian vehicles but also cars from Germany, Poland, France and the United States.

Learn about how the automobile evolved over the years. Many of the vehicles on display come from the early twentieth century and even earlier.

See the first vehicle Fiat produced in 1899 plus a Bernardi automobile from 1893. View a fully restored Benz Viktoria from 1893. It is one of the oldest vehicles still in existence anywhere in the world. See how its carriage-like design and large wheels fit well with one of the earliest engines ever produced.

Look at the beautiful 1928 Isotta Fraschini Tip 8A. This iconic luxury vehicle is also the same one featured in the classic film Sunset Boulevard.

#32 Explore Ancient Egypt at the Museo Egizio

See one of the world's largest collections of Egyptian artifacts at the Museo Egizio. This museum in Turin features more than 30,000 pieces. Many of these pieces were acquired in the early nineteenth century and continue to be on display today.

Walk into the Temple of Ellesyia, one of the largest surviving rock-cut temples still standing. The temple was moved from Qasr Ibrim to Turin to keep it from falling into a nearby lake. The inside walls feature carvings and indentations where people would pay their respects to various Egyptian gods.

Review the papyrus collection and see how hieroglyphics were first produced. The documents were used for centuries as a means of figuring out what the symbols meant.

Notice the copies of the Book of the Dead on display here. This important book was used by Egyptians to assist a person into the afterlife. It contains many spells that Egyptians used and ceremonial instructions to help guide deceased spirits on their way to the next world. The strong symbolism used throughout the book is vital to the development of the beliefs people around Egypt held. Interestingly enough, some people have requested that the Book of the Dead not be displayed because they fear it produces negative energy. Such requests have not been heeded.

Chapter 6 – Venice

Venice is one of the most intriguing cities in Italy. It is built on many islands around the Adriatic Sea. The canals are among the most popular places around Venice, but there are many other things to do while in the city beyond just enjoying a good boat ride. Then again, you would certainly have to get on a boat to reach a few of the more popular spaces around the city.

The city has a strong history to it as it is where many prisoners would be taken to serve their sentences or to be executed. While such activities do not take place here today, the city continues to be a vital window into the history of Italy.

#33 Enjoy a Ride Under the Rialto Bridge at the Grand Canal

One important feature of Venice is that it features a series of canals instead of roads. The canals are beautiful thoroughfares that link people around the many Gothic and Renaissance palaces and buildings that populate Venice.

But it is the Grand Canal that is the most familiar of these bodies of water. While in Venice, take a ride on the Grand Canal by gondola or water taxi.

Travel nearly two and a half miles along the Grand Canal as it snakes its way along the waterway. Start around the Santa Lucia rail station and head your way over to San Marco, the original space where the city's government was situated at.

Look at the beautiful houses and palaces that surround the Grand Canal as you sail along. Notice the distinct churches with their spires standing out along the entire canal.

The most important part of the Grand Canal is the Rialto Bridge. Travel under the bridge as you are on a gondola or taxi ride. The stone arch bridge features several arches on its main body. See how the arches are formed and produce a strong body all the way around.

#34 *Walk Along the Bridge of Sighs*

The Bridge of Sighs is one of the more popular bridges in Venice. This bridge was built in 1600 as a connection between the prison and Doge's Palace.

The bridge is named for how many prisoners who were transported over it could be heard sighing. This bridge marked the last shot of Venice that prisoners would see before they were sent to their places of punishment.

See the beautiful look of the main canal from across the Bridge of Sighs as you stand on it.

Watch for gondolas as they move through the area.

Look at how intricate some of the stone grills around the bridge are designed. The grills were prepared to keep the light that gets into the bridge from being too strong.

#35 Enter Doge's Palace on the Waterfront

Doge's Palace is one of the more distinctive buildings in Venice to see. The fourteenth-century building has a detailed number of arches around its outside. The intricate façade has been duplicated by many architects around the world.

The immaculate design of Doge's Palace makes it look as though it is floating in the middle of the water. The design exhibits the strong power and influence of the building. It is here where the leader, or doge, of Venice, resided centuries ago. Prisoners would be sent here for sentencing with some of them being executed in the building.

Tour the site and see many of the secret walkways and doors surrounding the building. Notice the intense amount of detail used in getting the building organized while keeping the walkways private and secure. This was all done to keep the walkways from being exposed to the public, thus ensuring people would not try to escape or find ways to rescue prisoners.

See some of the sights around St. Mark's Square while out here too. Doge's Palace is not too far from the square, thus placing it in the middle of one of the busiest spots in the city.

#36 Explore a Napoleonic Site in the Academy Gallery

Napoleon established an academy for academic studies in Venice in 1807. Over time the property was converted from a place of study into an art museum. This is what the Academy Gallery in Venice is like today.

See the Renaissance art pieces around the gallery. The pieces come from the fourteenth to eighteenth century for the most part. Various works by Titian and Tintoretto are on display with many of these depicting scenes from the Bible.

The most iconic piece on display is the Vitruvian Man, a 1490 marking by Leonardo da Vinci. The drawing was designed to illustrate what constitutes the ideal proportions for the human male. Much of this is inspired by architecture and from the philosophies of Vitruvius, a Roman architect.

The measurements of the Vitruvian Man continue to be studied to this day. It is symbolic of the strong planning and architectural concepts that da Vinci established in his work.

Be advised though that the Vitruvian Man paper is not always on display. Because of its fragile nature, this and other items of its kind are often kept in storage and are subject to extensive restoration procedures. Contact the Academy Gallery before you get here to see if the Vitruvian Man is actually on display.

#37 Visit the Markets at St. Mark's Square

St. Mark's Square is a major meeting space for people around Venice. The square is right around where Doge's Palace and other important sites in Venice are located.

Enjoy watching the people go by as you spend a bit of time at St. Mark's Square. The diverse population traveling around the area makes for a fascinating sight worth watching.

Take in a meal at one of the restaurants around the square or shop at one of the special boutiques around the region. The area is popular for housing many markets that offer special souvenirs, art pieces and foods from all around Venice. Look for gondola hats here but do shop around; all of the retailers around the place sell their own hats with each being made with different standards in mind. Compare each option to see which gondola hat is right for you to bring home.

Try heading to this place early on in the day or during the late evening hours. The spot tends to get very busy during the daytime. Be prepared to bring your money as well. The stops at the markets are varied based on what they offer, but they tend to charge more money than most other places in Venice, what with there being more people heading out to this area.

#38 Watch a Show at the Teatro La Fenice

When you walk indoors into the Teatro La Fenice, you will notice a beautiful look with red velvet chairs and gold linings around the space. The fact that these features are still intact to this day is impressive given how the theater suffered from two major fires in its history.

First built in 1792, the Teatro La Fenice burned down twice. The first burned down in 1836 but was rebuilt and opened a year later. The second case occurred in 1996 although the acoustics were saved. The theater was eventually rebuilt and reopened in 2004.

The Teatro La Fenice is also known as the Phoenix as it is a theater that continues to rise even as it is destroyed. The venue is important to the history of opera as it is where many operatic premieres took place including works by Bellini and Verdi.

Visit the theater and take a tour of this extensive venue. Enjoy a seat on one of the luxurious red velvet chairs. Get a view of the golden accents all around the theater. Notice how well the colors mix in with each other. See some of the Renaissance-inspired art pieces on the ceiling as well.

See the impressive detail that comes with the chandelier. The unit is modeled after the original one that was used in the first incarnation of the theater.

Look at the calendar of events to see what is coming to the theater. Traditional Italian opera is the most popular type of event to see here. Some dance and classical music performances are held at the venue as well. Be prepared to wait for tickets though as there are only a thousand seats in the theater. Some of the best seats, particularly many of the boxes, cost a sizeable amount of money for you to get tickets for as well.

Chapter 7 – Naples

Naples is a city in the southern part of Italy. The city is one of the oldest in the world as people have lived here in many forms since at least the second millennium BC.

The city has thrived over the years and has especially recovered in the later part of the twentieth century. The city was the most heavily bombed part of Italy during World War II. Over the years Naples has rebuilt itself into an important cultural haven. The city has some of the most beautiful markets in the country.

#39 Explore the Past at the Naples National Archeological Museum

Start your trip to Naples at the National Archeological Museum. Walk inside the old building that was constructed as a cavalry barracks in the late sixteenth century.

The museum focuses on Roman, Greek and Egyptian art pieces. It includes artifacts from the cultures which delve into how the region developed and how people lived.

View the Farnese marble sculptures around the museum. These include various productions from famed Greek sculptor plus some Roman copies of Greek works. Interestingly enough, some of the Roman copies are the only surviving ones of some of the older Greek pieces from Nesiotes and Calamis among others.

Observe the famous Farnese sculptures of Hercules and Atlas. These two are the inspirations for how people see these figures to this day. Notice how Atlas is kneeling with a celestial sphere over his shoulders and not the planet Earth. Review the immense detail of the Farnese Bull, one of the largest sculptures on display.

Discover the mosaics that were recovered from the nearby city of Pompeii. The Alexander Mosaic is the most famous of these. The art piece features a depiction of Alexander the Great and his army going into battle with Persian forces.

View the Egyptian collection featuring thousands of old items gathered from archeological digs around the country. A fully preserved mummy is on display here.

#40 Go Shopping At Christmas Alley
Italy is home to many attractive public markets, but not many are as distinct as Christmas Alley.

This venue in Naples is an outdoor shopping area that sells small art pieces of all kinds.

Check out the attribute statuettes, ornaments, and other small items all around. Many of the products around Christmas Alley include ornaments that you could place on your Christmas tree, hence the name of the market.

Ornaments of all kinds can be found around here. Everything from religious figures to more contemporary items can be found here. Most of these products are made by locals and are hand-crafted with an emphasis on very specific details and designs.

The markets are made with many products in mind, but the values of these products will vary based on who you contact. You can try to negotiate deals with some places although it is not always easy for you to make this work.

Enjoy a good drink and some gelato while at Christmas Alley. A few cafes are found around the entire space. Such places add more of a natural and local flair to the experience you will come across.

#41 Shop at the Via Caracciolo e Lungomare Promenade

Head to the seaside and visit the Via Caracciolo e Lungomare promenade. See many vendors and cafes all around as they serve fine drinks and meals and sell numerous arts and crafts products.

Enjoy walking along the promenade as you go to various attractive shops. See the nearby island of Capri from across the sea. Look for Mount Vesuvius in the background. You can even order a water taxi to take you from one part of Naples to the next.

Do be careful when heading out here though. Some of the artisans at the promenade are notorious for being rather tough on people. That is, they do not take no for an answer all that easily. You might have to say no to them two or three times just to get them off your back. Of course, the odds are you might find some great gifts at the promenade, what with the region being filled with so many attractive shops.

#42 See the Veiled Christ at the Sanservo Chapel Museum

The Sanservo Chapel is a late-sixteenth century church that has been converted into an art museum. View the various art pieces and sculptures around the museum. Look at the two anatomical exhibits that feature old corpses that were plastered and preserved for analytical and display purposes. The models are designed with many metal materials to display how the human body operates by basing them off of the bodies of actual deceased people.

The most iconic part of the museum is the Veiled Christ sculpture. Prepared by Giuseppe Sanmartino, the sculpture features a depiction of

Jesus after his death. Notice how the shroud covers his body while his facial features can be seen protruding from it. His crown of thorns and many other instruments used in his death can be seen near his feet.

The Veiled Christ sculpture is an important piece of art to those of the Catholic faith. It depicts Jesus in one of his most important moments. The sculpture was crafted with immense detail and is one of the most outstanding features to look at while in Naples.

A quick note: Naples is indeed not too far off from Mount Vesuvius and the city of Pompeii. The two take a bit of extra time for you to get there from Naples. A little more detail on Pompeii will be covered later in this guide.

Chapter 8 – Verona

The city of Verona is located off of E70 right in between Milan and Venice. The city has developed a strong reputation for being the place where William Shakespeare's famed tragedy Romeo and Juliet takes place in.

It is with this fact in mind that Verona is one of the most popular places to visit while in Italy. It is a romantic city with many beautiful sights worth spotting.

#43 Experience Shakespeare's Inspiration at the Casa di Giulietta

Travel to Via Cappello no. 23 while in Verona to see a fourteenth century stone house that is believed to be where the Capulet family of the play lived. See the Casa di Giulietta, the area where one of the most important scenes in the story was inspired by.

Notice the balcony outside the courtyard at the house. The balcony is considered the place where Juliet stood as Romeo professed his love for her.

See the bronze statue of Juliet in the courtyard. Touch the right breast of the statue. Legend has it that those who touch the right breast will become lucky and fall in love someday.

Write your name on the wall heading into the entrance. Legend states that those who write their names on the wall will attain everlasting love that will never be broken.

You could also write the names of you and your true love on a lock and attach it to the gate at the back left part of the house. This is another symbolic gesture showing that your love will never be broken.

Many letters come into the Casa di Giulietta every year. Thousands of people, mostly women, write letters to the house expressing their desire for love. This includes a hope for falling in love with someone and having a love that will never be lost. Leave your letter to Juliet at the gate.

#44 Get to the Top of the Torre dei Lamberti

Climb the spiral staircase to reach the top of the Torre dei Lamberti. At around 275 feet in height, it is one of the most prominent buildings in Verona.

This tower was built in the late twelfth century. Notice how marble materials have been added around the building to reinforce its structure. Some of the marble was added after 1403 when the top part of the building was hit by lightning.

Also, see how detailed the spiral staircase is as you walk up on it. The staircase is distinct for its fascinating appearance as you look down.

See the two bells at the tower. The Marangona bell signals the hour of the day and also sets off if a fire is spotted. The Rengo bell calls the population over to the city council or tells the public to take up arms. The bells are not necessarily used to signal fires or to tell people to take up arms although the other regular commands are highlighted.

#45 See Opera at the Arena di Verona

When you head to the Arena di Verona, you will notice how it has a look similar to the Roman Colosseum. While the venue did host many games when it first opened in 30 AD, the venue has since changed to become an amphitheater.

See an operatic performance at the Arena di Verona. With seating for nearly 15,000 people, you will surely find a spot to catch a show at.

You are guaranteed to enjoy the amazing sights and sounds of an operatic show. The Arena di Verona is designed with some of the best acoustics of any such venue.

Various Italian operas have been performed including Carmen and Aida. Most of the shows take place in the summer months when the weather is ideal for performances.

Look to see if any popular music acts are coming to the arena. The venue has become popular for modern music shows thanks to its appealing design and its ability to carry sounds well. The venue has hosted many acts from all corners of the world including Paul McCartney, Whitney Houston, Pink Floyd, Rod Stewart, Pearl Jam, Radiohead and Leonard Cohen.

Chapter 9 – Other Places Around Italy

There are many other intriguing sights to see and things to do as you travel around Italy. These include things that are well outside some of the more significant cities in the country.

Some of these attractive spots are located around islands just off of the mainland. Water taxi and ferry services are available to and from these islands.

#46 Enjoy the Wines of Piedmont

The Piedmont region is one of the most beautiful places in Italy to visit. Located near the borders with France and Switzerland, the region is famous for being home to the communes of Barolo and Barbaresco. These two villages are considered to be the most important spots for wine in Italy.

Enjoy the views of the rolling meadows where vineyards are planted, and grapes are harvested every day for wine production. The farms utilized extremely high standards for growing their grapes, a point that is heavily inspired by the nearby French vineyards.

Look at the Nebbiolo grape as it grows around Piedmont. The Nebbiolo grape is a red wine grape native to the area. It has a full body with a highly acidic tone that adds to the flavor of the wine.

Take in a fine dinner at one of the wineries around the region. Enjoy a quality wine from one of the many wineries based out of Barolo or Barbaresco. Such places as Casa Sobrero, Damilano, Socre, Cigliuti, Castello di Verduno and Paolo Manzone are among the best wineries to enjoy while out here. Don't forget to visit the local wine museum highlighting the evolution of the wine industry in Italy and how it continues to grow today.

Also, be sure to enjoy some fine baked bread at one of the wineries. These bread products go perfectly with olive oil that has been freshly pressed. Many of the wineries have their own olive plant spaces where olives are harvested and pressed for their oils every day. The oils and bread go perfectly with the wines you will enjoy out here.

#47 Visit the Island of Sicily

The island of Sicily is the most noteworthy island in Italy. It is off of the southern end and is situated in the middle of the Mediterranean Sea. Visit the island and explore everything it has to offer.

Enjoy the nightlife and beaches around the island. Head to the Mazzaro or Fontane Bianche beaches and relax on the white sandy shores.

Go to the western end of the island and visit the city of Palermo. Take in the evening at one of the clubs or restaurants around the space. Travel a little further to the west to the Castello di Venere, a twelfth century Norman fortress along the shore. This fortress was built on top of an old Roman temple.

#48 See Where Napoleon Lived on Elba

From 1814 to 1815, Napoleon was exiled to the Italian island of Elba. Travel to this island on the western shores of Italy to see where he lived.

Tour the Villa Napoleonica, the house that he was based in during his exile. Visit the museum to see artifacts relating to his life and his time in Italy. Learn about how he took control of much of Europe and how his empire and rule fell apart over the years.

After visiting his old sites, climb up to the top of Mount Capanne. It is around 3,000 feet in height. The island is around the western end of the island. Look at the top of the mountain and see the waters and many scenes around Elba.

Notice as you walk along Elba how peaceful and quaint the area is. The island was chosen as a place to exile Napoleon at as a means of keeping him from being active or a threat in some way. The quiet spaces around Elba and the picturesque scenes of the area are beautiful. Of course, these are places that Napoleon would not have enjoyed, what with him being heavily limited over what he could do.

#49 Watch Your Step At the Leaning Tower of Pisa

Take a walk up to the top of the nearly 180-foot-tall Tower of Pisa while in the Tuscan city of Central Italy. Pisa is a beautiful city home to many important churches and various scenes all around the Arno river. The city is even home to a university founded by Napoleon. But what makes the city famous more than anything else is its distinct tower that has officially become known to many as the Leaning Tower of Pisa.

The Tower of Pisa was not necessarily designed to lean as it does. The construction of the tower began in 1173 and continued until 1372. The foundation of the tower was too weak. It was only around ten feet deep. The subsoil was also unstable and unable to handle the weight of the tower.

Fortunately, the soil did eventually settle to keep the tower from falling over. The soil settled as construction was halted due to ongoing battles within the Republic of Pisa against other regions in the area.

Today the tower leans about 3.97 degrees to the side. This creates a very noticeable tilt when you view the tower from a distance. You will also notice a slight sensation as you walk along the tower. Keep your hands on the rails around the top part of the tower.

Notice as you climb up the tower that one side of the upper floors is a little taller than the others. This is to offset the tilt and to create a curved look.

See the seven bells inside the bell chamber within the tower. Each of the bells represents a single major note in the musical scale.

As you get closer to the tower, notice how one side has a series of lead counterweights at the base. These were applied to limit any possible shifting. The building was confirmed to be fully stabilized in 2008 and is estimated to remain stable until at least the early part of the twenty-third century. This gives you more than enough time to visit the Leaning Tower of Pisa and climb up to its top.

#50 *Climb Up One of the Mountains At the Pennine Alps*

The Pennine Alps are right on the northwestern end of Italy. The mountains go along Italy and Switzerland and make up a key western part of the Alpine mountain range.

The mountains around the Pennine Alps include some of the most beautiful spaces you could climb up. These include many that are at least ten thousand feet in height.

Lyskamm is the tallest of these mountains situated in Italy. It is around 14,800 feet in elevation at its peak. It is a dynamic mountain that is typically reached from the west to the east as it is a safer route that is less likely to experience possible avalanches.

The Matterhorn is around the same height and is distinct for its symmetrical look. Its base is easily accessible by rail.

You would have to contact a charter group for information on climbing up one of these mountains if you are interested. Check with such a group to see what gear is required, an itinerary for getting up to one of the mountains and any safety points that must be followed. Also, you might want to get a physical before you travel to see that you can actually handle the high elevations of some of these mountains or even be able to climb one of these mountains in general.

It can also take a few days for you to get up to one of these mountains. A typical trip up to a mountain could take five to ten days depending on where you are climbing and the strategy used for getting up to the summit. Contact a charter group that could help you with planning a trip to one of these mountains for added details on what you could get into.

#51 See the Active Volcano on Stromboli

Stromboli is an island near the southern end of Italy not too far off from Sicily. It is part of an arc of volcanic islands around the Tyrrhenian Sea. The island is also home to the mountain of the same name. Mount Stromboli is one of the few active volcanoes in existence around Italy.

Watch as fumes come out of the volcano from afar. The volcano regularly has small eruptions. The fumes are easily visible throughout the day.

Do not try to go too far close to the volcano. Although it is only around 3,000 feet in height and technically easy to climb, it is dangerous as there is always a potential for a major eruption to take place. The risk is a major part of why only about 500 people live on the volcanic island.

Watch for scientist crews around the island as they measure the volcano's eruptions. Gas analysis systems can be found all around the island. These measure the intensity of the gases produced by the volcano.

Bonus - #52 Enjoy the Nightlife of Capri

Go off of the mainland not too far from Naples and enjoy the sights and thrills around the island of Capri. It is a prominent island that has become a major resort destination.

Enjoy visiting some of the natural bird habitats around the island. Capri is popular among birding enthusiasts as several species can be found. The peregrine falcon, woodcock, and quail are among the more popular birds to find here.

See the Blue Grotto while traveling along the island. The cave is noted for the beautiful blue colors people see through the holes of natural light that move into the region.

Don't forget to spend a good evening out on the island. The resorts are home to many clubs and dance halls where people party the night away.

Be sure to wear your Capri pants while on the island. The pants were named after the island for being relaxed in their appearance.

Bonus - #53 Ski At One of the Northern Resorts

Perhaps you want to enjoy the mountains of Italy, but you really do not have a desire to climb one of them. There are many famous Italian resorts around the northern end of the country that deserves to be seen.

Get to the northern end of the country to visit one of many attractive ski resorts around the region. Enjoy the Courmayeur resort and see the sights by cable car. Visit the historic church at the Madonna di Campiglio resort. Relax at one of the pools along the Canazei resort.

Whatever place you head to, you will find many skiing trails around the northern part of the country. Enjoy skiing out here and have fun going down the paths.

Many resorts have trails for beginners and experts alike. Most spots also have skiing schools. Take a few classes at one of these schools to learn how to ski. You will love the thrill that comes with skiing after you are finished learning how to get out on the slopes.

Some of these resorts come with a few additional attractions that add to what you can do while traveling. Rock climbing surfaces can be found around Campitello di Fassa and Sexten, for instance. You could also enjoy a hike around one of the appealing long distance trails along the Santa Cristina Gherdeina or Cavalese resorts.

For the best experience, head out to one of these resorts in October or November. These are times when the weather is chilled enough for skiing while the snow conditions are comfortable. They are also points where traffic around the resorts is not all that strong.

Bonus -#54 Relax at the Waters Around Lake Garda

Go outside Verona to one of the largest bodies of water in Italy, Lake Garda. The lake is around 30 miles in length. They are surrounded by many mountains including some of the nearby Dolomites.

With many shores and resorts around Lake Garda, you are bound to enjoy a relaxing time. The region is popular for its quaint shores and attractive spaces that are beloved by tourists and locals alike.

Enjoy sailing or windsurfing around the northern end of the lake. The north is ideal for such activities as the winds are a little stronger up here.

See a few of the historic sites around Lake Garda. Look for the site of the Battle of Rivoli, a 1797 battle during Napoleon's French campaign. See the town of Salo where Mussolini established his capital for the Italian Social Republic in the 1940s. This was a place used by German troops during World War II as an outpost for communications and planning.

Travel around the lake to see the sites where the Battle of Solferino took place. This was held in 1859 during the Second Italian War of Independence. The fight between Italy and Austria left nearly a quarter of a million people dead and produced conditions that were so disturbing that it eventually led to the formation of the International Red Cross and the drafting of the Geneva Conventions, treaties relating to how people are handled in war that are still utilized to this day.

Bonus - #55 See the Ruins of Pompeii

It is only appropriate that the last thing to do while in Italy is to see where one civilization met its untimely end. Go not too far from the Bay of Naples to the city of Pompeii, an old city that was destroyed in 79 AD.

Pompeii was built in the seventh century BC and was home to nearly 10,000 people. It had its own water system and theater among other places to keep the city functional.

But in 79 AD, the nearby volcanic mountain Vesuvius erupted, destroying the city and killing the people who lived there. The massive amounts of ash killed the people living there.

As you tour the ruins, you will notice that many of the spaces around the landscape have been carefully preserved. These ruins were secured because of a lack of air and moisture in the region for generations. The city was considered lost for nearly 1,500 years before it was eventually found in 1599 and then excavated in further detail in the mid-eighteenth century.

Notice the Temples of Jupiter and Apollo, two vital meeting spots, in the ruins. Look at the walls to see pieces of art that were carefully preserved over the years. The frescos around the area include scenes of life at the time and what people enjoyed doing for a living in the region.

Look at the Indian art pieces and sculptures that were collected from the ruins. The people who lived in the city had strong trade connections with India at the time.

See the plastic casts scattered around the ruins. These casts were produced to get ideas of where the people were when they died and the positions they were in. Since the area has remained untouched for so long, the attention to detail around the region is immaculate.

Conclusion

Italy is one of the most iconic countries in the world. The sights and sounds of the country have amazed people for generations. It is no secret that the country is one of the most popular ones in the world for people to visit.

The mountains and islands of Italy and its many cities are home to some of the most attractive spots you could ever visit. Whether you are interested in art or shopping or you just want to relax, the odds are you will find something to do in the country.

As you travel through Italy, you will see the history of the world come to life. You will find many cultural features that make it one of the world's most distinct places to visit. The fact that everything has been preserved so well over the years only makes Italy all the more intriguing of a country to visit.

Use this guide to help you figure out what you can do when visiting Italy. As you look around, you will see that there are many things worth exploring as you visit this distinct country.

Still, this is only a small sampling of the things you could do while in Italy. The extensive history and culture of Italy make it a memorable space.

Have fun looking around Italy and seeing everything it has to offer. From seeing some of the most beautiful structures in the world to taking part in many activities that people around Italy like to do, you will have a memorable time in the country.

Made in the USA
Lexington, KY
12 December 2017